Original title:
Interplanetary Insanity

Copyright © 2025 Creative Arts Management OÜ
All rights reserved.

Author: Nolan Kingsley
ISBN HARDBACK: 978-1-80567-825-0
ISBN PAPERBACK: 978-1-80567-946-2

Madness in the Stars

A comet slipped on banana peel,
It spun around, oh what a wheel!
The aliens danced with glee and cheer,
In their disco ship, they saw no fear.

Mars wore a tutu, twirling bright,
While Saturn laughed at a meteor's flight.
Pluto played tag with a passing star,
And they all laughed, forgetting who they are.

Galactic Laughter

Jupiter told a joke so slick,
His moons all groaned, 'Oh, that was quick!'
Venus chuckled in a gas-filled haze,
While Mercury winked through the cosmic maze.

Asteroids rolled on the stellar floor,
Singing tunes that shook the core.
With every bounce, they spread their cheer,
In this vast void, no one shed a tear.

Unruly Orbits

Neptune's rings were in a spin,
As space krakens joined in the din.
Galaxies tangled in a wild waltz,
Around black holes filled with goofy faults.

The sun wore shades to block out the rays,
Sipping fusion drinks while it blazed away.
Stars peeked out, wearing silly hats,
Cosmic chaos with galactic spats.

Fractured Lightyears

Shooting stars raced just for fun,
Chasing laughter till the night was done.
A wormhole hiccuped in a cosmic breeze,
Spitting out oddities with utmost ease.

Quasars blinked with a cheeky grin,
While time wobbled like a panicked tin.
In the great expanse, all seemed absurd,
As aliens giggled without a word.

Celestial Riddles

A Martian twirls in a purple skirt,
With moon rock shoes, oh what a flirt!
Jupiter jokes with a comet so spry,
While Saturn laughs, rings clapping high.

Venus throws pie, a sugary flight,
While Pluto sips lemonade, feeling light.
Cosmic giggles orbit the stars so bright,
With aliens dancing through the cosmic night.

The Space Giggle

A rocket with wheels rolls down the lane,
Chasing a star that forgot its name.
Cosmic cats play with lights from afar,
Swapping their tails for a bright shooting star.

Asteroids bouncing, what a fine sight,
Wobbling and wobbling, no end in sight.
In the vacuum, they crack jokes so loud,
At the punchline, even a black hole's proud!

Brown Dwarf Daze

A brown dwarf yawns, feeling quite lazy,
While space ants march, oh so crazy!
Galactic snails take their time with flair,
Leaving trails of glitter through the thin air.

Dancing gas clouds, swirling in cheer,
With tales of mischief, they gather near.
A nebula giggles, tickling the void,
In this dazed cosmos, boredom's destroyed!

Beyond the Event Horizon

A wormhole opens, drinks on the deck,
With aliens laughing, what the heck!
Beyond the horizon, time takes a spin,
As everyone tries to fit all their kin.

Jokes echo loudly in the fabric of space,
With light-speed laughter, oh what a race!
Around a black hole, they twirl and they prance,
In this wacky cosmos, there's always a chance!

Asteroids of Ambiguity

In a belt of rocks, they spin and sway,
Dodging and weaving in a silly ballet.
One claims it's a car, while another's a cat,
Who knew space rocks could be such a prat?

Toasters zoom by, on a cosmic spree,
They're arguing over who stole the tea.
Asteroids giggle, a peculiar sight,
As they dance with the stars, till the morning light.

Nebular Nonsense

In clouds of gas, where dreams take flight,
Unicorns roam, in colors so bright.
They gossip about comets with tails like a kite,
And sing silly songs in the dead of night.

Planets are prancing, in clownish parade,
Making moonbeams laugh, as if they were played.
Oxygen chuckles, while hydrogen beams,
In this wacky universe, bursting with dreams.

Cosmic Conundrum

A riddle unfolds, in the depths of space,
With aliens dancing, in a nutty race.
They can't find their hats, or their shoes, oh dear!
They trip on stardust, but still persevere.

With telescopes twisting, they spy on the Sun,
Arguing over who's having more fun.
While black holes giggle, and white dwarfs snicker,
In this cosmos full of joy, everything's quicker.

Reality Bends Beyond Mars

Past the rusty red, where dreams go bizarre,
Lies a town of robots, named Quirkylah Star.
They brew up some mischief with metal so grand,
And sip on their soups, with a fork and a hand.

Teleporting turtles, in a cosmic game,
Racing through galaxies, just to find fame.
Gravity giggles, and time starts to twist,
In a world where no talent can ever be missed.

Cosmic Dreamscape

In the void where giggles roam,
Planets dance like they're at home.
Stars wear hats made of spaghetti,
Meteors bounce, oh so ready!

Galaxies swirl in cotton candy,
Asteroids chuckle, feeling dandy.
Little aliens play hopscotch,
While comets plot a silly botch.

Gravity's slip, a cosmic prank,
Jupiter's moon gives a cheeky wink.
Saturn's rings toss confetti high,
As space cows drift, mooing by.

Beyond the sun, where laughter glows,
Nebulas twist in goofy flows.
In this realm of endless jest,
The universe puts humor to the test.

Chaotic Cosmic Winks

Planets play tag in a slinky line,
Starlit jesters sip moonlight wine.
With each flash, a nod, a laugh,
Galactic pranks, a silly path.

Wormholes yawn, a cosmic snore,
While black holes plot to steal the chore.
Celestial squirrels chase shining nuts,
Warp speed winks in hurried struts.

Meteors roll like bowling balls,
Lunar puppies leap and bawl.
Comedy reigns on cosmic stages,
While planets flip through cosmic pages.

A spaceship filled with clowns and jest,
Zooms past comets, no time for rest.
In this wild and whirling spree,
Who knew space could be so free?

Whims of the Universe

Stars dance like they've lost a bet,
Planets spinning in a cosmic jest.
Galaxies twirl in a haphazard way,
While moons giggle and laugh at the play.

Comets zoom by, with cotton candy tails,
Asteroids roll like they're telling tales.
The universe chuckles, a bright, shining face,
In this wacky, wild, outer space race.

Stranded on Saturn

Oh dear, I'm stuck in the rings of a gas,
Where clouds of ammonia swirl and pass.
The locals are funky, with three eyes and fluff,
They say, 'Earthling, you've had enough!'

They juggle the storms and wear hats made of light,
While I sip on some lemonade, feeling alright.
But finding a ride back to home is a twist,
As I slide on the ice, in a cosmic mist.

The Martian Maze

Red dust rises in a dizzying spin,
While playing tag with a Martian twin.
We're weaving through canyons, oh what a race,
With gummy bears as our snack in this place!

The rover's our ship and it bounces with glee,
As we shout cosmic secrets, just him and me.
We laugh 'til we snort, as we flip over rocks,
In this maze of adventure, with giggles in flocks.

Echoes of Extraterrestrial Eccentricity

From Venus, they send us bubblegum cheer,
With aliens dancing, they twirl and disappear.
They play hopscotch on clouds made of stars,
While sipping on bright drinks from Martian bars.

Galactic karaoke, the songs are a riot,
With one-eyed creatures—we can't help but try it!
A chorus of croaks, and a cacophony loud,
In this wacky place, we sing terribly proud.

Cosmic Fireworks

In space where stars ignite,
Aliens dance in glee,
Shooting sparks from every side,
It's quite a sight to see.

Planets spin in silly twirls,
With comets in a race,
Little green men pull their curls,
In this wild cosmic place.

Galaxies toss their hats,
As they trip on cosmic rays,
Gravity forgets the spats,
And joins in all the plays.

So grab your space suit tight,
Enjoy the cosmic spree,
When fireworks burst at night,
The universe roars with glee.

Stars Collide in Laughter

A supernova's silly song,
Echoes through the night,
With asteroids all dancing along,
Creating pure delight.

Stars collide with big old grins,
Like bumpers in a game,
They knock and jolt, and round they spin,
But there's no one to blame.

Moonbeams giggle, playful lights,
As meteors whiz around,
Funny faces, cosmic sights,
Make the universe astound.

In this vast and zany ball,
Where whimsies come alive,
The laughter echoes, through it all,
As cosmic dreams arrive.

Beyond the Cosmic Veil

Through the veil where dreams take flight,
Jokes ripple past the stars,
Space-time folds with pure delight,
Winking at Jupiter's cars.

Rockets wear outrageous hats,
As they zoom and spin,
Mars grins wide, it doesn't chat,
But loves the cosmic din.

Neptune tickles, Saturn sings,
With rings that whirl and twirl,
Galactic giggles are the things,
That make these worlds unfurl.

So come and join this silly crew,
In laughter, we will sail,
For in this cosmos, skies are blue,
Beyond the cosmic veil.

Black Hole Burlesque

Deep in space, a dance unfold,
Around a black hole's crest,
Stars strip down, both brave and bold,
And give their cosmic best.

Neutron stars with twinkling spins,
Waltz in fuzzy light,
Spinning tales of silly sins,
In a cosmic laugh-off fight.

Supermassive just holds the song,
As black holes sway and sway,
Creating fun that can't go wrong,
In this absurd ballet.

So let's embrace this strange spree,
With giggles in our quest,
For in the folds of mystery,
Is the black hole burlesque.

Astral Reveries

In a spaceship made of cheese,
Martians dance with playful ease.
Stars hum tunes of silly rhyme,
Galactic pranks in endless time.

Jupiter laughs in swirling hues,
While Saturn's rings sing silly blues.
Floating cows on comet trails,
Tickling aliens in their gales.

Moonbeams wear outrageous hats,
Chasing tiny, giggling rats.
Pluto's icy smile so wide,
As rocket ships take off with pride.

Cosmic jokes in endless flight,
In a world that feels just right.
With a wink and twirl we find,
In this madness, joy combined.

Lunatic Orbits

Dancing stars in swirling whirl,
Galaxies spin and giggle, twirl.
Martian pies are flying high,
While spacecats meow and sigh.

Asteroids serve the wobbly drinks,
While Earthlings give bewildered winks.
Quick! Grab a space taco treat,
Before it zips right from your seat.

Venus plays the ukulele,
As Pluto paints the night so fray.
Floating fishes, purple-green,
In these orbits, joy's obscene.

Galactic laughter fills the air,
With flying ducks and cosmic flair.
Join the fun 'neath starry skies,
Where every nutty thought complies.

Fractured Galaxies

In twisted space where time is bent,
Kooky creatures burst, content.
Neon boots stomp funky beats,
As gravity slips, our joy repeats.

Silly robots clown around,
Making music, no care found.
With wobbly legs and giggly grins,
They spin around, let chaos win.

Black hole parties never cease,
Where wisps of jokers find their peace.
Galactic hiccups, comic blunders,
In this realm of funny wonders.

Stars play poker with the moons,
As aliens dance to jolly tunes.
In laughter's grasp, we all unite,
In fractured galaxies, pure delight.

Wraiths of the Void

Ghostly figures float and sway,
Tickled by the Milky Way.
In a soup of wobbly light,
They prank the asteroids at night.

Ethereal chuckles fill the dark,
As shooting stars make their mark.
Wraiths of whimsy, full of jest,
In the void, they never rest.

With jellybeans from Mars' core,
They play hopscotch by the shore.
Invisible games, oh what fun,
Chasing shadows, they all run.

Floating in this cosmic sea,
Where laughter reigns, wild and free.
In the madness, we find a jam,
With wraiths enjoying every slam.

Interstellar Surrealism

In a spaceship made of cheese,
Aliens dance with the breeze.
They juggle stars with a grin,
While the moon plays violin.

Comets wear polka dot hats,
And Pluto's a cat that chats.
With a wink and a twirl,
They orbit in a whirly swirl.

Gravitational Guffaws

Asteroids bowling through space,
Stars giggle and lose their place.
Galaxies tease with their spin,
While black holes suck in a grin.

Saturn's rings spin like a top,
Bouncing balloons make it stop.
Laughing comets burst into light,
As Mars throws a party tonight.

Cosmic Quake of Reason

A meteor tripped on a star,
Shouting, 'I'm not going far!'
While Venus made silly faces,
Jupiter danced in bright spaces.

Nebulas wore silly wigs,
As they played with cosmic jigs.
They scribbled dreams in the sky,
With laughter that made comets fly.

Quantum Whirl

Electrons spin like a top,
In a world where logic can flop.
Quarks tease with a little twist,
It's a dance you can't resist.

Photon parties at light speed,
Jumping, tumbling like a seed.
With laughter echoing through time,
And craziness kept in rhyme.

Orbiting Lunacy

In a spaceship made of cheese,
The aliens dance with ease.
Spaghetti trails behind their feet,
As they twirl to a funky beat.

Planets giggle, stars shoot beams,
Cosmic pranks fuel wild dreams.
Martians juggle comet tails,
While Venus sends them spicy quails.

A rocket fueled by fizzy drinks,
Bounces over Saturn's kinky kinks.
Laughter echoes through the void,
In chaos, never once annoyed.

Black holes wink with cheeky grins,
As UFOs steal cosmic spins.
Who knew space could be this wild?
A universe of joy, like a child!

Daydreams Across Dimensions

Llamas float in twilight skies,
With rainbow wings and silly ties.
They sip the stars from glowing cups,
While Jupiter hops and magically puffs.

Through wormholes filled with candy canes,
Silly creatures play like loony trains.
Galaxies spin, a merry-go-round,
Where giggles in the stardust abound.

Socks from space rain down like bliss,
Aligned with every fluffy kiss.
Time tickles in a jester's way,
Dancing quietly without a say.

And if you find a space cat's hat,
Just tip your own and give a pat.
Across dimensions full of cheer,
Each daydream sings a cosmic sphere!

Adrift in the Asteroids

Floating rocks with silly faces,
Bouncing 'round in dizzy chases.
They chuckle in a metal ballet,
While comets wink in bright array.

An octopus spins a hula hoop,
While meteorites form a jumping troop.
Laughing, they tiptoe on starlight beams,
Chasing all their wacky dreams.

Galactic jellybeans abound,
As quirky quirks spin round and round.
Spaceships made of shiny gum,
Zooming through the cosmic hum.

Asteroid fields like dance floors fair,
With cosmic critters in the air.
Adrift in light, they're full of glee,
In this wild, wobbly jubilee!

Galactic Whimsy

A squirrel navigates the void,
With acorns as his fleet deployed.
He juggles moons with tiny paws,
While space whales clap with gleeful jaws.

Dancing on the rings of Saturn,
Balloons float with a giggly pattern.
Aliens wear polka-dot suits,
As stars serve up their cosmic fruits.

The sun wears shades, it's quite a sight,
While planets throw a wild night.
Cosmic cake with sprinkles bright,
Brings everyone pure delight.

Through every twist and wacky bend,
The universe will always lend,
A hug, a laugh, a funny quirk,
In galactic realms that joyfully work!

The Dance of Distant Worlds

In a galaxy far, they twirl and spin,
Jupiter's got rhythm, let the dance begin!
Saturn rings in laughter, what a silly sight,
Mars does the cha-cha under cosmic light.

Pluto's in the corner, sipping space tea,
Winking at the stars as they jiggle with glee.
Venus steals the spotlight, twirling with flair,
While Earth laughs out loud, tossing sparkles in the air.

Nebulae Fantasies

In clouds of colors, they play hide and seek,
With supernova giggles, so loud, so unique.
Comets zoom past, with frisbees in tow,
While stardust confetti begins to bestow.

Wormholes stretch wide for a cosmic race,
Uranus grins widely, 'I'll win this space chase!'
Asteroids chuckle as they tumble and roll,
In this whimsical void, they all share a soul.

Astral Antics

The sun plays peek-a-boo behind a bright star,
While aliens laugh, saying, 'Look at them spar!'
Neptune's blue giggles ripple through the dark,
As Martians juggle moons, what a wild lark!

Galaxies whirl like a silly ballet,
With each twist and twirl, they shout, 'Hooray!'
In the void of night, friendship is the key,
In this zany cosmos, we're all full of glee.

Disorder Among the Planets

Mercury races round with a wacky grin,
Causing chaos, where to even begin?
With Venus taking selfies, all glammed and bright,
And Saturn's lost rings are a comical sight.

Galactic pranks soar through the endless dark,
As Martian comedians leave a humorous mark.
The moon's double-daring, not one to be shy,
While black holes chuckle, 'Oh, we'll never die!'

Phantom Moons

In a land where stars wear hats,
Silly critters dance with bats.
Jupiter's got a pizza place,
Served by aliens with a smiley face.

Mars tried out some juggling skills,
But dropped its rocks; oh what thrills!
Venus laughed, spilled all her tea,
And said, "Space parties are wild, you see!"

Echoes of Misadventure

A comet flew right past my nose,
I yelled, "Watch out!" as it froze.
Galaxies giggled at my fright,
As they twirled in the cosmic night.

Neptune wore a polka-dot coat,
While Saturn rode a spacey boat.
They raced around in cosmic loops,
Making music with starry hoops.

Celestial Capers

Eating stardust on a whim,
When Uranus tried to sing a hymn.
His voice echoed through the void,
And made black holes ever so annoyed.

Asteroids rolled in a silly game,
Playing tag with comets, such fame!
Each crash caused a burst of light,
Creating a disco ball in flight.

Extravaganza of the Exosphere

Out in space where dreams collide,
Aliens skate on solar tide.
They twirled with grace, and giggled loud,
While shooting stars cheered, oh how proud!

A rocket broke into a dance,
Launching astronauts with a prance.
Floating high, they began to sing,
In this wild cosmic fling!

Infinite Spiral Delusions

In a spaceship made of cheese,
We zoom past stars with ease,
Dancing with space cows, oh what a sight,
Singing off-key into the night.

Aliens giggle, they've got our song,
Join the chorus, it won't take long,
Floating through dreams and candy bars,
We lose our minds amongst the stars.

Planets waltz in a cosmic race,
While space squirrels keep up the pace,
Juggling comets, what a grand show,
We laugh 'til our cheeks start to glow.

Lost in the twist of a spiral theme,
All is a wild and wacky dream,
As cosmic giggles fill the air,
We spin and twirl without a care.

Galactic Shenanigans

A penguin pilot with shades on bright,
Flies through the cosmos, what a delight,
Spinning in circles, he can't help but dance,
Chasing stardust, giving luck a chance.

Martians play hopscotch on asteroids round,
While silly sound effects make strange sounds,
Giggles erupt in the great black expanse,
As Saturn's rings join in the prance.

Comets pass by with a wink and a tease,
Trading their tails for a slice of cheese,
Laughter echoes from moon to moon,
In this celestial, zany afternoon.

Stars wearing hats, all dressed for fun,
Galactic mischief has just begun,
We'll rollick and race till the day is done,
In this universe, we all are one.

Black Hole Ballads

There's a hole in space that swallows it whole,
Where jokes get lost, playing a role,
A giggling tyrant that eats every line,
And burps out stardust that sparkles and shines.

Singing to planets who spin all around,
They snap their fingers to the crazy sound,
"Hey, black hole!" they yell with glee,
"Keep the party going, you're the key!"

Inside this vortex, a wild jam's grown,
Where lost socks and whispers find a home,
So grab your microphone, no need to be shy,
Join the black hole's choir, let your spirit fly.

While the universe spins, oh what a scene,
Fuzzy creatures dance where the light has been,
Each ballad a wink, each note pure charm,
In the depths of chaos, we're safe from harm.

The Lost Satellites' Lament

Floating adrift in cosmic despair,
Lost satellites wander, searching for fare,
With antennas all tangled, they've shed quite a tear,
"Oh where are the orbits we once held so dear?"

They spin in circles, each has a tale,
Of planets they hugged and adventures set sail,
With signals gone crazy, they chatter and roam,
"Please find us a planet we can call home!"

With humor unending, they laugh 'til they're sore,
For space is a circus, forever in lore,
While meteors zip by, wishing them well,
Their voices resound like a glorious bell.

In the vastness of space, they'll dance through the night,
With dreams of their journeys now taking flight,
For anchored or free, they know they belong,
In the laughter of starlight, they'll always be strong.

Starry-Eyed Euphoria

In a rocket made of cheese,
Zooming past some silly peas,
Dancing with the laughing stars,
Juggling planets, cosmic bars.

Saturn's rings are just a game,
With space cats who stake their claim,
Orbital giggles, cosmic cheer,
In this realm of floating beer.

Asteroids scream, but it's all right,
For we dance till the morning light,
Wormholes twist with jokes so grand,
In this wild and wacky land.

Aliens sing a quirky tune,
Underneath the laughing moon,
Pluto winks, a cheeky sprite,
Join the fun, it's quite a sight!

The Whimsical Milky Way

Galaxies swirl like cotton candy,
With comet tails that smell quite dandy,
Fluffy clouds of stardust fluff,
Crack a joke, it's never tough.

Meteors zoom with silly faces,
Playing tag in cosmic spaces,
Riding rays of joyful light,
What a marvelous delight!

Nebulae dance in vibrant hues,
Painting skies with candy news,
Space penguins sliding down starlines,
Sharing laughs and cosmic signs.

Astro-balloons float up high,
Holding dreams that touch the sky,
Where every laugh and giggle grows,
In this realm where humor flows!

Spheres of Insanity

In the craziness of space so wide,
Planets giggle, stars collide,
Floating fish in zero G,
Make for quite the sight, you see!

Twirling moons with silly hats,
Chasing shadows of the cats,
Galactic parties, wild and free,
Join the fun, come laugh with me!

Time is warped, so don't be late,
Jokes discovered on a plate,
Galaxies spin in joyful spree,
Singing tunes of lunacy.

Every sunbeam has a jest,
Every black hole hides a fest,
In these realms of wild delight,
Find your madness, dance all night!

Fantasia Beyond Pluto

Beyond Pluto, where odd things dwell,
Octopus astronauts ring the bell,
Singing songs of jellybeans,
In this land of wacky scenes.

Celestial clowns in spacesuits dance,
Jumping high, they take a chance,
Hydrogen balloons float and sway,
In the cosmos where we play.

Mars wears shades, and Venus grins,
Rocket rides and moonlit spins,
Galactic fun, a vibrant show,
With a twist the universe knows.

In the stars, we share a laugh,
With space whales as our other half,
Join the ride, the fun's insane,
In this fantastic cosmic campaign!

Chaotic Constellations

Stars are dancing, what a sight,
Planets twirl in wild delight.
Saturn's rings jump rope in space,
While comets make a silly face.

Uranus giggles, oh so loud,
While Jupiter boasts, feeling proud.
Mars trips over a moonlit crater,
Screaming, "Help! I need a waiter!"

Nebulae burst with colorful flair,
Aliens juggling without a care.
Galaxies clash in a comic brawl,
Painting the cosmos, a vivid sprawl.

Pulsars laugh while asteroids sing,
Creating a joy that all might bring.
In this madcap sky, let's all unite,
To share the laughter of pure starlight!

Astronaut's Anarchy

Floating snacks in zero-g,
Spaghetti noodles flirt with me.
Tangled hair and floppy shoes,
Orbiting chaos is the muse.

Spacesuits bursting at the seams,
Dreaming big of cosmic dreams.
Oops! My coffee's now a cube,
Zipping past the earthen lube.

Gravity takes a much-needed break,
As astronauts bake a moonlit cake.
Oven's broken, dough in the air,
As aliens join, their giggles rare.

Lost in laughter, we all collide,
Riding rockets, our pride won't hide.
In this madness, joy we weave,
With gravity gone, you must believe!

Celestial Whirlwinds

Satellites spin like tops of joy,
While cosmic winds toss a lost toy.
Meteor showers bring silly cheer,
Rain down laughter, loud and clear.

A whirlwind of dust, a comet's tail,
Spins in circles, like a happy snail.
Orbs of gas puff out like cheeks,
While cosmic critters play hide and seek.

Eclipses cause an uproar loud,
As shadows dance and zigzag, proud.
Laughter echoes through the dark,
Creating treats like a bright spark.

With every swirl, we can't sit still,
In this craziness, we find our thrill.
Join the dance in this stellar show,
Where joy takes flight and stars brightly glow!

Cosmic Jesters

Galactic clowns in polka dot ships,
Riding solar winds with silly flips.
Comets honk their horns so bright,
Shooting stars burst into laughter's light.

Black holes spinning a playful tale,
Swallowing things without a fail.
Jupiter's moons throw a party wide,
With alien guests, dancing side by side.

Martian mimes in a cosmic play,
Their silent antics brighten the day.
With laughter echoing through the night,
Even the dark gets a joyous light.

Cosmic jesters of the grand design,
Turning the universe into a line.
With giggles ringing from star to star,
In this funny realm, we'll go far!

Space Oddities

In a rocket made of cheese,
Martians dance with whimsical ease.
Silly hats and moonlit skies,
Catch a glimpse of their wild eyes.

Aliens play hopscotch with stars,
Juggling planets in candy bars.
Zany sounds from afar do beckon,
While space cows moo in galactic wrecks.

NASA's lost a sock or two,
Floating in space, just like your shoe.
Astronauts giggle in zero G,
As they chase their own feet, oh me!

Comets wear polka dot wraps,
As aliens nap in cosmic laps.
Space pranks echo in nebulae,
A universe that laughs on high.

Celestial Circus

Underneath the starry dome,
Clowns juggle asteroids like foam.
Elephants float on fluffy clouds,
While aliens cheer in wild crowds.

Trapeze artists swing on light,
Daring leaps in the endless night.
A ringmaster with a twinkling beam,
Commands the space with a gleeful scream.

Cotton candy made of stardust,
Balloons that once were cosmic rust.
The cosmic carousels spin with glee,
While astronauts dance with crabby bees.

Tickets bought with meteorite dust,
Laughing loudly is a must.
So grab a seat and take a ride,
In this circus where the stars collide.

Dark Matter Madness

In a realm where shadows prance,
Dark matter brings a silly dance.
Ghostly giggles fill the void,
Where gravity plays tricks and toys.

Stars play hide and seek with light,
While comets don their costumes bright.
Giant black holes trap a joke,
A cosmic pun, or so we hope.

Wormholes burst with laughter loud,
As spacetime bends — a laughing crowd.
Hitchhikers with a grin and hat,
Ride on beams, just imagine that.

Einstein winks and gives a nod,
As cosmic jesters all applaud.
In the abyss of the unknown,
Madness reigns — the stars now moan.

Lunatic Lunars

On the moon where sillies thrive,
Lunatics in shorts arrive.
Craters filled with giggles bright,
As they play tag in the pale light.

Bouncing high with silly glee,
Zero gravity sets them free.
They build castles made of fluff,
Riding meteors, just for fun!

Napping under stars that twinkle,
While cosmic squirrels play a sprinkle.
Telescope beanies are the style,
As they enjoy a moonlit smile.

Candy comets drift on by,
They reach for sweets as echoes sigh.
Lunatics under a lunar glow,
Laughing softly in a cosmic flow.

Gravity's Fool

Floating high in silly suits,
Chasing dreams like shooting roots.
Asteroids wear hats of cheese,
While comets dance with cosmic breeze.

Zany voices from afar,
Barking orders like a star.
Laughter echoes in the void,
As gravity's game is joyfully toyed.

Spinning tops on Martian soil,
Juggling moons, it's pure uncoil.
Galactic giggles fill the air,
Whirling dervishes of cosmic flair.

Planets play peek-a-boo so sly,
Crying out, "Look, I'm the starry guy!"
With every twist and every dance,
We find our way in this cosmic romance.

Tesseract Tangents

In a box that bends and twirls,
Chasing lights like dizzy pearls.
Every angle a wiggly prank,
With dimensions that bloom and tank.

Wormholes wrap in silly spins,
As laughter starts where math begins.
The shapes are bizarre, yet so divine,
Creating puzzles in a straight line.

Colorful blobs with squiggly lines,
Squeak like mice, but are playing pines.
Tesseracts with disco lights,
Twisting time in crazy flights.

In this maze of fun and folly,
Let's laugh at geometry, oh so jolly!
Through the folds of space and time,
We dance to a wobbly rhyme.

Psychotropic Planets

Planets puffing clouds of fizz,
Sailing spaceships, what a whiz!
Jupiter plays on a giant swing,
As Saturn strums its rings and sings.

Neptune's filling cups with dew,
While Mars makes pizza for the crew.
Venus is blushing, it's quite a sight,
Running wild in colors bright.

Uranus giggles, feels a breeze,
Dancing 'round with cosmic ease.
Each star a cheeky little sprite,
Bouncing joy in the endless night.

Galaxies swirl with laughter's grace,
Creating smiles across the space.
So let's embrace the cosmic cheer,
In this wacky universe, never fear!

The Nebulous Nonsense

In clouds of fluff and starry dust,
We spin the tales of cosmic trust.
Silly beings in a cosmic race,
Finding treasures in empty space.

Wobbling worlds flip like pancakes,
Crafting giggles with every quake.
Celestial clowns toss suns like balls,
Comets zoom past with fizzy calls.

Mars wears shades, oh what a sight,
While moons play tag, both day and night.
Black holes spinning tales of jest,
In this nonsense, we're all blessed.

Let's chuckle at this cosmic lore,
With stars that wink and planets snore.
In the vast, surreal expanse,
We find the joy, the cosmic dance.

Supernova Somersaults

In a galaxy so vast, they spun with glee,
Stars doing cartwheels, wild and free.
Planets laugh like children, oh what a sight,
Galactic giggles echo through the night.

Whirling meteors on a cosmic spree,
Sassy asteroids roll up with tea.
Cosmic clowns drift in a playful race,
With twinkling mischief painted on their face.

Neon comets slide on rainbow trails,
Jupiter's jester tells outrageous tales.
Black holes chuckle, pulling all near,
In the carnival of space, bring on the cheer!

Wobbling moons dance with a buzz,
Shooting stars join in, what a fuzz!
Across the void, they leap and bounce,
In this vast playground, laughter pounce!

Eclipsed Euphoria

When the sun plays hide-and-seek with the moon,
Laughter erupts like a funny cartoon.
Saturn's rings giggle, spinning rings of pranks,
While friendly space dust fills the colorful ranks.

Planets wear shades, a stylish parade,
Cosmic confetti, a glittery cascade.
Asteroids waltz in a haphazard glance,
Creating wild steps in a chaotic dance.

Neptune's pools pop with a splash of fun,
While Martian frogs leap under the sun.
Galaxies swirl, in a jovial chase,
In this comical dance, the universe's grace.

Jumping aliens join the sunlit spree,
With goofy hats and wild jubilee.
Through the void, they bounce and sway,
In eclipsed joy, they frolic and play.

Ethereal Chaotic Dances

Through the cosmos, a wacky waltz,
Stars twinkling bright, with giggles that pulse.
Ethereal beings in silly attire,
Jiving and jiggling, never tire.

Galactic sparklers spin and twirl,
Creating light trails that swirl and whirl.
Planets join in, with funky moves,
Setting the rhythm, the fun grooves.

Space whales hum silly tunes so sweet,
While neutron stars tap their cosmic feet.
Mischievous sprites scatter bright gleams,
In this madness of memes, they live their dreams.

Wobbling orbs take a break to rest,
High-fiving meteors, it's truly the best.
In this galaxy of laughter and prance,
The universe revels in a chaotic dance!

Comet's Carefree Madness

A comet zooms with a comic flare,
Trailing sparkles, dancing in the air.
Chaotic joy streaking past the sun,
In this playground of stars, it's all in fun.

With a flick and a spin, it spins around,
Riding the waves of a joyful sound.
Alien ducks in spacesuits glide,
Chasing the comet on a crazy ride.

Laughing rings bridge Saturn's fun,
While errant moons play peekaboo in the sun.
Every orbit's a reason to cheer,
Cosmic capers bring the universe near.

On this journey, each tickle and tease,
Fills the cosmos with joyous ease.
Through the solar systems, they dart and dash,
In the light of a comet, it's a laughter flash!

Cosmic Whirlwinds

In a space ship made of cheese,
We zoom past stars with joy and ease.
Alien cats are chasing tails,
While one-eyed frogs tell silly tales.

Planets wobble, spin, and glide,
As comets sip their cosmic ride.
Saturn wears a tidy ring,
And Neptune plays a ukulele string.

Moonbeams dance upon a breeze,
Whirling past a group of trees.
Galaxies gather for a game,
While meteorites roast marshmallow flames.

We giggle through the cosmic mess,
Finding humor in the stress.
In this universe of glee,
Join the laughter, wild and free!

Stars on the Brink

Twinkling stars play hide and seek,
While asteroids decide to sneak.
One star fell with a comical thud,
And landed right in a puddle of mud.

Jupiter's got a giant grin,
Laughing at the chaos within.
Pluto shouts, 'Hey, I'm still here!'
But no one can see him, oh dear!

Space whales swim in wobbly lines,
Singing tunes of awful pines.
Galactic giggles fill the air,
Making even black holes stop and stare.

Shooting stars drop by for tea,
Sharing tales of cosmic spree.
If you catch one, make a wish,
For a dance with an alien fish!

Nebulae of the Mind

In the galaxy of wacky dreams,
Creatures dance in funny streams.
Thoughts explode like supernovae,
Where giggles grow and wisdom roves.

Moons wear hats of polka dots,
As cosmic bloopers form big knots.
Nebulas swirl with colors bright,
While robots play chess every night.

Black holes yawn, 'We need a break!'
Pushing thoughts with a cosmic shake.
Ideas bounce like rubber balls,
Echoing through the cosmic halls.

So let your fancy take the stage,
Silliness is all the rage.
In this dreamy, stellar kind,
Find the giggles in your mind!

Celestial Carnival

The carnival of space is here,
With rides that spin and folks to cheer.
Gravity-defying hula-hoops
Keep the astronauts in joyful loops.

Clowns in spacesuits jump and dive,
As starry balloons begin to thrive.
Cotton candy made of stardust fluff,
Every bite is silly and rough.

Flying saucers race around,
While alien musicians make a sound.
Juggling planets, round and bright,
Creating laughter in the night.

So come aboard this cosmic fest,
And leave behind all of the rest.
In this carnival of delight,
Every moment's a funny sight!

Chaotic Cosmos

In a galaxy swirling with oddities bright,
Cows in spacesuits take leisurely flight.
Aliens dance on neon-lit moons,
While robots hum nonsensical tunes.

Planets are jammed with jelly and cheese,
Sailing on beams of whimsical breeze.
Comets are racing in flip-flops and shades,
Shooting through space with giddy parades.

Asteroids chuckle, they roll and they spin,
As Martians play poker, and blue men all grin.
Galactic gumballs explode in delight,
Bouncing off stardust and glowing night.

With each cosmic hiccup, a strange giggle grows,
Galaxies burst into wacky shows.
The laughter echoes across the vast sea,
Of the shimmering, silly, celestial spree.

Eclipsed Realities

Planets in pajamas spin tales of the night,
While space squirrels throw pillows in cosmic delight.
Suns wear sunglasses, looking quite cool,
And comets zoom by, making a pool.

Silly stardust storms tickle the stars,
While dreamers invent interstellar cars.
Galactic tomatoes roll down moon hills,
Tickling all beings with cosmic thrills.

In the void, there's a band of strange cats,
Singing with joy, wearing big top hats.
Licorice lightning and gumdrop trees,
Wobble through space on a breeze that tease.

The universe wobbles with laughter and glee,
As creatures invite us for soda and tea.
Nothing makes sense in this whimsical spree,
A cosmic joke, oh how funny can be!

Spheres of Delirium

In a dance where the planets play hooky from school,
Spaghetti meteors splash in a shimmering pool.
Galaxies painted in polka dots bright,
Twirl in a jig under cotton candy light.

Astrological clowns juggle stars with finesse,
While sheep in the cosmos throw parties, no stress.
The Milky Way's filled with bizarre brain games,
Where portraits of penguins all wear funny names.

Cosmic pie fights erupt with sweet goo,
As beings from Pluto join in the brew.
Each solar system has its own quirky flair,
Of burbling bubbles and inflatable air.

With laughter transcending the void and the space,
The absurdities mock us with light-hearted grace.
Galactic giggles are phenomena rare,
In the spheres of delirium, we float without care.

Stellar Hysteria

With logic bamboozled by whimsical whims,
Planets converse while the starlight swims.
Jazz hands of Jupiter sparkle and sway,
While comets engage in a funky ballet.

The moons wear bow ties, serving cosmic pies,
And octopus astronauts leap through the skies.
Velcro asteroids stick to bizarre dreams,
Creating a ruckus with giggles and screams.

Space-time's a circus with creatures galore,
Dancing through dimensions, a bright, crazy tour.
Eclipsing logic with laughter's delight,
In stellar hysteria, everything's bright.

With Neptune in sneakers and rings full of bling,
The universe chuckles at everything.
Floating in madness, yet bursting with cheer,
A joyful reminder that laughter is near!

Planetary Paradoxes

In a world where cows can fly,
The sun wears shades, oh my!
Mars drinks soda, stars sip tea,
And Jupiter's juggling a puppy tree.

Saturn's rings are hula hoops,
While Venus dances with funny troops.
Uranus laughs at the cosmic show,
As Mercury just tripped on a toe.

Pluto claims it's a big deal,
Says it's the king of cosmic zeal.
But it's just a dog with a funny hat,
Trying to impress a moon-shaped cat.

Galaxies swirl like a soup so thick,
While asteroids play an old-school trick.
Floating around in a shiny bus,
Yelling, "Who needs gravity? Not us!"

Comets of Confusion

Comets streak with tales absurd,
While aliens dance and sing in herds.
One wears a tutu, the other a suit,
Throwing a party, oh what a hoot!

Stars blink twice, then wink in delight,
Creating a ruckus in the night.
Planets spin with a giggle and cheer,
As Neptunes' bubbles float near.

Asteroids play a crazy game,
Whoever lands last is never the same.
They hide in craters, laugh out loud,
Joining forces with the comet crowd.

Uranus tries to sing a tune,
While the moons bounce like a cartoon.
They'd win an award for cosmic fun,
In the galaxy's race, they surely won!

Orbiting Absurdity

In a spin, oh what a sight,
Moonbeams chase the stars at night.
Mars wears pants, what a disgrace,
While Saturn's rings keep up the pace.

Giant robots dance in line,
Sipping rocket fuel with a twist of lime.
They pirouette without a care,
While comets burst through cosmic air.

Neptune's pets are all made of cheese,
Floating around with utter ease.
They giggle, they chirp, a merry band,
Spreading joy through the cosmic land.

Galaxies spin in dizzying loops,
Causing laughter among the groups.
Oh dear stars, what a comical plight,
As they tumble through endless night!

Twisted Gravity

Gravity's gone on a wild spree,
Planets bouncing with glee.
Jumping jupiters, leaping star,
Even the sun's got a funky guitar!

Rockets dance like they've lost their mind,
While curious comets playfully grind.
Black holes chuckle, "Join the dance!"
As particles swirl in a cosmic trance.

Floating forks and spoons abound,
Weird creatures twirl all around.
Planetary pranks are all the rage,
While stars turn the night into a stage.

Cereal orbits in a bowl,
Milk and stars taking a stroll.
Dancing through space, what a surprise,
With cereal moons and milky skies!

Starlit Surprises

In a spaceship made of cheese,
We zoom past stars with ease.
A squirrel piloting, quite absurd,
Chasing comets, isn't it weird?

Asteroids dance, they wear a hat,
While aliens play with a giant cat.
They sip on drinks of purple hue,
Squeaking laughs, 'Come join our crew!'

Moonlit moons roll down the lane,
While lollipops fall like rain.
Underneath a disco ball,
We twirl and spin, just having a ball!

Galaxies giggle, a cosmic joke,
A planet sneezes, up goes the smoke.
Each starlit wink brings a surprise,
In this madcap realm, joy amplifies!

Astral Reverie

In a realm where gravity's shy,
Dancing cows leap and fly.
The sun wears shades, quite a sight,
While stars twinkle in pure delight.

Jellybeans float in rainbow streams,
As kittens play with space-bound dreams.
With silly hats on every face,
We chase the meteor shower race.

Floating boots and candy canes,
Conducting symphonies with strange refrains.
Planetary pranks abound,
In the echoes of laughter, we're joyfully drowned!

Space-time giggles, what a treat,
As clocks spin fast on their own beat.
In this reverie of the absurd,
Every moment's wild, every thought's a word!

Cosmic Carnival

Roll up, roll up, come take a ride,
On a comet that's more like a slide!
Ferris wheels made from cosmic zest,
A funhouse that won't let you rest.

Cotton candy clouds tempt the bold,
With fireworks bursting like tales of old.
Dancing robots in polka dots,
Joining us in delight-filled knots.

Wormholes that spin and tickle your nose,
While space-fish giggle in sparkly clothes.
Each twist and turn, such vibrant glee,
A cosmic carnival for you and me!

As laughter echoes through the stars,
We crunch on snacks from Mars.
In this wild ride, sorrows are light,
The universe's humor shining bright!

The Unhinged Universe

Galaxies wobble like a drunk on the run,
Twinkling like they've seen too much fun.
Planets giggle, they can't sit still,
In this unhinged space, time has no will.

A black hole wraps around a joke,
As comets whoosh by, puffing smoke.
With every twist the cosmos leaks,
Logic's lost in these crinkled peaks.

Saturn's rings throw a pie in the air,
While space cows float without a care.
Meteor showers raining pies,
In laughter, there's no room for sighs.

Silly stars spark a giggling jest,
In this universe, we find our rest.
The unhinged cries may bellow and roar,
But joy erupts, who could ask for more?

Void of Clarity

In a space where socks go lost,
Planets spin with wild exhaust.
Stars wear hats of mismatched style,
While comets dance and mock a smile.

Galaxies swirl like a smoothie blend,
With jellybeans they seem to send.
Asteroids toss confetti high,
As aliens chuckle by and by.

Gravity plays a game of tag,
While spacecrafts zoom with a zig and zag.
Neon lights flash, a disco scene,
In this void, all's quite obscene.

Jupiter wears a polka-dot tie,
While Saturn's rings give a twinkling sigh.
Laughter echoes in a silent space,
In the void, it's all a giggling race.

Whirling Halos

Underneath the swirling stars,
Martians ride in candy cars.
They twirl and spin with endless glee,
While Pluto waves, 'Come share with me!'

Venus boasts a garden cheer,
Full of veggies that end up here.
Mars flips pancakes at the dawn,
While space cows jump on the lawn.

The sun wears shades, a stylish ray,
As rockets play hide-and-seek all day.
Nebulas giggle in vibrant hues,
As they throw around some sparkly blues.

With laughter echoing through void's embrace,
Whirling halos of joy we chase.
Galactic pranks in the cosmic play,
In this bizarre melee, we'll sway!

Time Warp Whimsy

Time jumps forward then slips back,
Like a kitten on a jolly track.
Wormholes wink with a cheeky nod,
As clocks spin 'round, oh what a prod!

Einstein rides a roller coaster,
With Newton shouting, "I'm the poster!"
Every minute's a peanut chase,
In this warped and wacky space.

Pulsars tickle with a fun quirk,
Light-years bounce with a goofy smirk.
Past and future flip like cards,
A cosmic giggle beneath the stars.

Through portals we skip and hop,
In this time circus, we won't stop.
With laughs that stretch from here to there,
In a whimsical ride, we'll dare!

The Cosmic Chaotic

In this realm where rules don't fit,
Black holes hide and comets split.
Galactic jests with silly tunes,
Dancing with all the twirling moons.

Aliens wear mismatched shoes,
While rocket ships brew cosmic blues.
Stars are chefs, cooking up dreams,
In saucers bubbling, or so it seems!

Chaos reigns in gravity's mess,
As Saturn's rings spin to impress.
The universe winks, a cheeky muse,
In this wild dance, we can't refuse.

From supernovas to kitten fights,
Every moment's filled with delights.
The cosmic laughter wraps us tight,
As we join this zany flight!

Tangents of the Unknown

In a spaceship made of candy bars,
Floating past the smiling stars,
Jupiter's giggles, Saturn's sighs,
We toast to the moon with fizzy pies.

Martians dance with glee and grace,
Wearing hats of outer space,
They serve up tacos filled with cheese,
While aliens laugh and sneeze like bees.

A comet zooms, a rocket farts,
As we play darts with glowing hearts,
Black holes invite for a wild ride,
Where laughter echoes, can't be denied.

So strap on tight, don't lose your grin,
As we spin in circles, let the fun begin,
For in this chaos, joy's the key,
In every tangent, come and see!

Starlit Bedlam

Underneath the shiny lights,
Space cats host their nightly fights,
With laser beams and fluffy toys,
They create mayhem; oh, such noise!

Zany creatures sing off-key,
Cosmic karaoke, pure jubilee,
The asteroids roll, can't help but laugh,
While meteors dance the wobbly staff.

We've got moon pies that bounce and fly,
On pizza comets; oh my, oh my!
Galactic clowns juggle stars with cheer,
Their jokes might make you shed a tear.

So join the fun, let loose your mind,
In this bedlam, joy's what you'll find,
Every star up there is quite absurd,
In starlit madness, nothing's deterred!

Gravitational Gambols

Round and round the planets race,
In a game of cosmic chase,
Friends with rings and jolly caps,
We tumble down in silly laps.

Gravity's a trickster, let's be clear,
It lends a hand, then disappears,
We bounce like balls on silly beams,
Floating through our wildest dreams.

Laughing stars throw glitter bombs,
While space-goats play their rhyming psalms,
Orbiting the funny side,
In this wacky world, let's confide!

So let's embrace this cosmic clip,
With pear-shaped moons and banana ships,
In gravitational joy we'll dwell,
In this madness, all is swell!

Dimensionally Distorted Dreams

In dreams where socks can dance and prance,
Galaxies take a backward stance,
Sock puppets lead the conga line,
In a multi-dimensional wobbly climb.

Twirling suns with hats of cheese,
Play hopscotch across the breeze,
Lunar llamas jump and shout,
In twilight realms where fun's about.

Riding rainbows, slipping through,
Chasing cows that moo in blue,
Time skips like stones in a pond,
In this odd place, we're truly fond.

So take my hand, let's soar through beams,
In this place of twisted dreams,
Where the serious fades in silly schemes,
In dimensions lost, laughter redeems!

www.ingramcontent.com/pod-product-compliance
Lightning Source LLC
Chambersburg PA
CBHW071848160426
43209CB00003B/463